# AN INSPIRATIONAL
# QUOTE A DAY

## Inspirational Quotes about Life

### M.PREFONTAINE

*HTTPS://TWITTER.COM/QUOTES4LIVINGBY*

*HTTPS://WWW.FACEBOOK.COM/QUOTESFORLIVINGBY/*

# INTRODUCTION

This is a book of some of the greatest inspirational quotes to help motivate the reader to be more positive about life and gain greater success and happiness as a result.

Words have a power and the thoughts encapsulated succinctly can be inspirational and motivate individuals to change their lives.

This book has one quote for every day of the year and I hope will prove useful, insightful and the quotes will resonate with you. It may be that one of these quotations will enable you to change your life for the better.

If you are interested in being informed about future quote book offers, please send your first name and email to;

mprefontainequotes@gmail.com

# CONTENTS

Introduction..................................................................................... III

JANUARY ............................................................................................ 1

FEBRUARY .......................................................................................... 9

MARCH............................................................................................... 17

APRIL ................................................................................................. 25

MAY.................................................................................................... 33

JUNE .................................................................................................. 41

JULY ................................................................................................... 49

AUGUST.............................................................................................. 57

SEPTEMBER......................................................................................... 65

OCTOBER ............................................................................................ 73

NOVEMBER.......................................................................................... 81

DECEMBER .......................................................................................... 89

One Last Thing................................................................................... 97

# JANUARY

## January 1

**You can never cross the ocean until you have the courage to lose sight of the shore.**

*Christopher Columbus*

## January 2

**Success consists of doing the common things of life uncommonly well.**

*Anon*

## January 3

**Yesterday is not ours to recover, but tomorrow is ours to win or lose.**

*Lyndon B. Johnson*

## January 4

**Opportunities don't happen, you create them.**

*Chris Grosser*

## January 5

**Everyone is a genius. But if you judge a fish by its ability to climb a tree, it will spend its whole life believing it is stupid.**

*Albert Einstein*

## January 6

**Successful people do what unsuccessful people are not willing to do. Don't wish it were easier, wish you were better.**
*Jim Rohn*

## January 7

**The moments of happiness we enjoy take us by surprise. It is not that we seize them, but that they seize us.**
*Ashley Montagu*

## January 8

**Things which matter most must never be at the mercy of things which matter least.**
*Johann Wolfgang Von Goethe*

## January 9

**To accomplish great things, we must not only act, but also dream, not only plan, but also believe.**
*Anatole France*

## January 10

**Little minds are tamed and subdued by misfortune; but great minds rise above it.**
*Washington Irving*

## January 11

**The most common way people give up their power is by thinking they don't have any.**
*Alice Walker*

## January 12

**A bird doesn't sing because it has an answer, it sings because it has a song.**
*Maya Angelo*

## January 13

**Remember that not getting what you want is sometimes a wonderful stroke of luck.**
*Dalai Lama*

## January 14

**You can't use up creativity.  The more you use, the more you have.**
*Maya Angelou*

## January 15

**The world as we have created it is a process of our thinking. It cannot be changed without changing our thinking.**
*Albert Einstein*

## January 16

**He who rejects change is the architect of decay. The only human institution which rejects progress is the cemetery.**
*Harold Wilson*

## January 17

**I alone cannot change the world, but I can cast a stone across the waters to create many ripples.**
*Mother Teresa*

## January 18

**The greatest mistake you can make in life is to continually fear that you will make one.**
*Elbert Hubbard*

## January 19

**Life isn't about waiting for the storm to pass. It's about learning how to dance in the rain.**
*Vivian Greene*

## January 20

**You don't have to control your thoughts; you just have to stop letting them control you.**
*Dan Millman*

# January 21

Why worry? If you've done the very
best you can, worrying won't make it
any better.
*Walt Disney*

# January 22

If I had asked people what they wanted,
they would have said, 'Faster horses'.
*Henry Ford.*

# January 23

A tiger doesn't lose sleep over the
opinion of sheep.
*Shahir Zag*

# January 24

Kindness is a language that the deaf can
hear and the blind can see.
*Mark Twain*

# January 25

One day your life will flash before your
eyes. Make sure it's worth watching.
*Gerard Way*

# January 26

Integrity is doing the right thing, even
when no one is watching
*C.S. Lewis*

## January 27

**I hated every minute of training, but I said, 'Don't quit. Suffer now and live the rest of your life as a champion'.**
*Muhammad Ali*

## January 28

**Pay attention to your enemies, for they are the first to discover your mistakes.**
*Antisthenes*

## January 29

**Being realistic is the most common path to mediocrity.**
*Will Smith*

## January 30

**We tend to forget that happiness doesn't come as a result of getting something we don't have, but rather of recognizing and appreciating what we do have.**
*Frederick Keonig*

## January 31

**We don't stop playing because we grow old; We grow old because we stop playing.**
*George Bernard Shaw*

# FEBRUARY

## February 1

Remembering that you are going to die is the best way I know to avoid the trap of thinking you have something to lose. You are already naked. There is no reason not to follow your heart.

*Steve Jobs*

## February 2

You can't get to a place that you don't believe exists.

*Anon*

## February 3

A pessimist sees the difficulty in every opportunity; an optimist sees the opportunity in every difficulty.

*Winston Churchill*

## February 4

The most difficult thing is the decision to act, the rest is merely tenacity.

*Amelia Earhart*

## February 5

We can't help everyone, but everyone can help someone.

*Ronald Reagan*

## February 6

If you do not hope, you will not find
what is beyond your hopes.
*St. Clement of Alexandra*

## February 7

You can't soar with the eagles if you
keep scratching with the chickens.
*Nancy Dornan*

## February 8

Life consists not in holding good cards,
but in playing those you hold well.
*Josh Billings*

## February 9

Live simply so that others can simply
live.
*Mahatma Gandhi*

## February 10

There's nothing you can't do if you
want it bad enough.
*Danielle Sibarium*

## February 11

Happiness is when what you think,
what you say, and what you do are in
harmony.
*Mahatma Gandhi*

## February 12

**Success consists of going from failure to failure without loss of enthusiasm.**
*Winston Churchill*

## February 13

**The only place where your dream becomes impossible is in your own thinking.**
*Robert H Schuller*

## February 14

**Our greatest weakness lies in giving up. The most certain way to succeed is always to try just one more time.**
*Thomas Edison*

## February 15

**I've had a lot of worries in my life, most of which never happened.**
*Mark Twain*

## February 16

**If you care very much what other people think, you will find that you are not one of the ones doing the thinking.**
*James Frey*

## February 17

**No matter what the situation, remind yourself "I have a choice".**
*Deepak Chopra*

### February 18

If we're growing, we're always going to
be out of our comfort zone.
*John C Maxwell*

### February 19

The will to win, the desire to succeed,
the urge to reach your full potential...
these are the keys that will unlock the
door to personal excellence.
*Confucius*

### February 20

I am the greatest, I said that even
before I knew I was.
*Muhammad Ali*

### February 21

If someone tells you, "You can't" they
really mean, "I can't."
*Sean Stephenson*

### February 22

Whatever you want to do, do it now.
There are only so many tomorrows.
*Michael Landon*

### February 23

Happiness often sneaks in through a
door you didn't know you left open.
*John Barrymore*

## February 24

**The foolish man seeks happiness in the distance, the wise grows it under his feet.**
*James Oppenheim*

## February 25

**The secret of getting ahead is getting started.**
*Mark Twain*

## February 26

**Experience is the child of thought, and thought is the child of action.**
*Benjamin Disraeli*

## February 27

**How wonderful it is that nobody need wait a single moment before starting to improve the world.**
*Anne Frank*

## February 28

**Minds are like parachutes – they only function when open.**
*Thomas Dewar*

## February 29

**The optimist sees opportunity in every danger; the pessimist sees danger in every opportunity.**
*Winston Churchill*

# MARCH

## March 1

**Everything you've ever wanted is on the other side of fear.**
*George Adair*

## March 2

**Always look at what you have left.
Never look at what you have lost.**
*Robert H. Schuller*

## March 3

**Success is the sum of small efforts, repeated day in and day out.**
*Robert Collier*

## March 4

**Either write something worth reading or do something worth writing.**
*Benjamin Franklin*

## March 5

**Things turn out best for the people who make the best of the way things turn out.**
*John Wooden*

## March 6

**Knowledge will give you power, but character respect.**
*Bruce Lee*

## March 7

**A chief event of life is the day in which we have encountered a mind that startled us.**
*Ralph Waldo Emerson*

## March 8

**A hero is no braver than an ordinary man, but he is brave five minutes longer.**
*Ralph Waldo Emerson*

## March 9

**An ounce of action is worth a ton of theory.**
*Ralph Waldo Emerson*

## March 10

**Build a better mousetrap and the world will beat a path to your door.**
*Ralph Waldo Emerson*

## March 11

**Enthusiasm is the mother of effort, and without it nothing great ever achieved.**
*Ralph Waldo Emerson*

## March 12

**Setting goals is the first step in turning the invisible into the visible.**
*Tony Robbins*

## March 13

**Successful people ask better questions, and as a result, they get better answers.**
*Tony Robbins*

## March 14

**The best time to plant a tree was 20 years ago. The second best time is now.**
*Chinese Proverb*

## March 15

**It is never too late to be what you might have been.**
*George Eliot*

## March 16

**Build your own dreams, or someone else will hire you to build theirs.**
*Farrah Gray*

## March 17

**The happiness of your life depends upon the quality of your thoughts.**
*Marcus Aurelius*

## March 18

**Life can show up no other way than that way in which you perceive it.**
*Neale Donald Walsch*

## March 19

Between the stimulus and response,
there is a space and in that space lies
our freedom and power to choose our
response. In our response lies our
growth and our freedom.
*Victor Frankl*

## March 20

The majority of us lead quiet,
unheralded lives as we pass through
this world. There will most likely be no
ticker-tape parades for us, no
monuments created in our honor. But
that does not lessen our possible
impact, for there are scores of people
waiting for someone just like us to
come along; people who will appreciate
our compassion, our unique talents.
*Leo Buscaglia*

## March 21

You don't have to be the best at
something. You just have to be the most
determined.
*Lauren Burns*

## March 22

A well-developed sense of humor is the pole that adds balance to your steps as you walk the tightrope of life.
*William Arthur Ward*

## March 23

The good life is a process, not a state of being. It is a direction not a destination.
*Carl Rogers*

## March 24

A man would do nothing if he waited until he could do it so well that no one could find fault.
*Cardinal Newman*

## March 25

The period of greatest gain in knowledge and experience is the most difficult period in one's life. Through a difficult period you can learn; you can develop inner strength, determination, and courage to face the problems.
*Dalai Lama*

## March 26

All truly great thoughts are conceived while walking.
*Friedrich Nietzsche*

## March 27

**Remember that failure is an event, not a person.**
*Zig Ziglar*

## March 28

**Man's mind, once stretched by a new idea, never regains its original dimensions.**
*Oliver Wendell Holmes Sr.*

## March 29

**A leader is a dealer in hope.**
*Napoleon Bonaparte*

## March 30

**If you change the way you look at things, the things you look at change.**
*Dr Wayne Dyer*

## March 31

**The problem is not that there are problems. The problem is expecting otherwise and thinking that having problems is a problem.**
*Theodore Rubin*

# APRIL

## April 1

So many of our dreams at first seems impossible, then they seem improbable, and then, when we summon the will, they soon become inevitable.
*Christopher Reeve*

## April 2

The main thing is to keep the main thing the main thing.
*Stephen Covey*

## April 3

The future has several names. For the weak, it is the impossible. For the fainthearted, it is the unknown. For the thoughtful and valiant, it is the ideal.
*Victor Hugo*

## April 4

Do not fear to be eccentric in opinion, for every opinion now accepted was once eccentric.
*Bertrand Russell*

## April 5

Don't wish it were easier, wish you were better. Don't wish for fewer problems, wish for more skills. Don't wish for less challenges, wish for more wisdom.
*Earl Shoaf*

## April 6

**We have a 'strategic' plan. It's called doing things.**
*Herb Kelleher*

## April 7

**You can't build a reputation on what you are going to do.**
*Henry Ford*

## April 8

**The few who do are the envy of the many who only watch.**
*Jim Rohn*

## April 9

**There are two ways to climb an oak tree. You can climb it, or you can sit on an acorn and wait for it to grow.**
*Anonymous*

## April 10

**You can always find a capable helping hand at the end of your own sleeve.**
*Zig Ziglar*

## April 11

**Be like a postage stamp. Stick to it until you get there.**
*Harvey Mackay*

## April 12

In any moment of decision, the best thing you can do is the right thing, the next best thing you can do is the wrong thing, and the worst thing you can do is nothing.

*Theodore Roosevelt*

## April 13

Failure cannot cope with persistence.

*Napoleon Hill*

## April 14

Talent hits a target no one else can hit; Genius hits a target no one else can see.

*Arthur Schopenhauer*

## April 15

There's a difference between interest and commitment. When you're interested in doing something, you do it only when circumstances permit. When you're committed to something, you accept no excuses, only results.

*Art Turock*

## April 16

A champion is afraid of losing. Everyone else is afraid of winning.

*Billie Jean King*

## April 17

That some achieve great success, is proof to all that others can achieve it as well.
*Abraham Lincoln*

## April 18

If your actions inspire others to dream more, learn more, do more and become more, you are a leader.
*John Quincy Adams*

## April 19

Just when the caterpillar thought the world was over...it became a butterfly
*English Proverb*

## April 20

Who dares wins!
*SAS Motto*

## April 21

Logic will get you from A to B. Imagination will take you everywhere.
*Albert Einstein*

## April 22

Poverty was the greatest motivating factor in my life.
*Jimmy Dean*

## April 23

**Don't raise your voice, improve your argument.**
*Anonymous*

## April 24

**Do one thing every day that scares you.**
*Eleanor Roosevelt*

## April 25

**Innovation distinguishes between a leader and a follower.**
*Steve Jobs*

## April 26

**Doing what you like is freedom. Liking what you do is happiness.**
*Frank Tyger*

## April 27

**It's hard to beat a person who never gives up.**
*Babe Ruth*

## April 28

**Dream as if you will live forever. Live as if you will die today**
*James Dean*

## April 29

The secret of all victory lies in the
organization of the non-obvious.
*Marcus Aurelius*

## April 30

Don't tell me the sky's the limit when
there are footprints on the moon.
*Paul Brandt*

# MAY

## May 1

**Vision without action is a dream. Action without vision is simply passing the time. Action with Vision is making a positive difference.**
*Joel Barker*

## May 2

**Once children learn how to learn, nothing is going to narrow their mind. The essence of teaching is to make learning contagious, to have one idea spark another.**
*Marva Collins*

## May 3

**Don't be trapped by dogma – which is living with the results of other people's thinking.**
*Steve Jobs*

## May 4

**Time is the coin of your life. It is the only coin you have, and only you can determine how it is spent. Be careful lest you let other people spend it for you**
*Carl Sandburg*

## May 5

**Don't aim for perfection, aim for success.**
*Eike Batista*

## May 6

**When you want to succeed as bad as you want to breathe, then you'll be successful.**

*Eric Thomas*

## May 7

**He who asks is a fool for five minutes, but he who does not ask remains a fool forever.**

*Chinese Proverb*

## May 8

**If we did all the things we are capable of, we would astound ourselves.**

*Thomas Edison*

## May 9

**The greater the artist, the greater the doubt. Perfect confidence is granted to the less talented as a consolation prize.**

*Robert Hughes*

## May 10

**Don't let what you cannot do interfere with what you can do.**

*John R. Wooden*

## May 11

**One finds limits by pushing them.**

*Herbert Simon*

## May 12

Once you have mastered time, you will understand how true it is that most people overestimate what they can accomplish in a year – and underestimate what they can achieve in a decade.
*Tony Robbins*

## May 13

Far and away the best prize that life offers is the chance to work hard at work worth doing.
*Theodore Roosevelt*

## May 14

You must either modify your dreams or magnify your skills.
*Jim Rohn*

## May 15

The first one gets the oyster the second gets the shell.
*Andrew Carnegie*

## May 16

Hire character. Train skill.
*Peter Schutz*

## May 17

**A calm sea does not make a skilled sailor.**
*African Proverb*

## May 18

**To win without risk is to triumph without glory.**
*Pierre Corneille*

## May 19

**Don't let the fear of losing be greater than the excitement of winning.**
*Robert Kiyosaki*

## May 20

**Those who say it cannot be done, should not interrupt those doing it.**
*Chinese Proverb*

## May 21

**Speak the truth, but leave immediately after.**
*Slovenian Proverb*

## May 22

**Confidence is contagious. So is lack of confidence.**
*Vince Lombardi*

## May 23

**Don't tell me the sky's the limit when there are footprints on the moon.**
*Paul Brandt*

## May 24

**The man who has no imagination has no wings.**
*Muhammad Ali*

## May 25

**Nothing is overly hard if you divide it into small jobs.**
*Henry Ford*

## May 26

**Ninety-nine percent of people believe they can't do great things, so they aim for mediocrity.**
*Tim Ferriss*

## May 27

**Discovery consists of seeing what everybody has seen and thinking what nobody has thought.**
*Albert von Szent-Gyorgyi*

## May 28

**It's what you learn after you know it all that counts.**
*Harry S. Truman*

## May 29

**The best way to have a good idea is to have lots of ideas.**

*Linus Pauling*

## May 30

**To arrive at the simple is difficult.**

*Rashid Elisha*

## May 31

**Picture in your mind a sense of personal destiny.**

*Wayne Oates*

# JUNE

## June 1

**Hofstadter's Law: It always takes longer than you expect, even when you take into account Hofstadter's Law.**
*Douglas R. Hofstadter*

## June 2

**You've got to get up every morning with determination if you're going to go to bed with satisfaction.**
*George Lorimer*

## June 3

**The only thing worse than being blind is having sight but no vision.**
*Helen Keller*

## June 4

**I am not a product of my circumstances. I am a product of my decisions.**
*Stephen Covey*

## June 5

**When I let go of what I am, I become what I might be.**
*Lao Tzu*

## June 6

**Education costs money. But then so does ignorance.**
*Sir Claus Moser*

## June 7

**Tough times never last, but tough people do.**
*Dr. Robert Schuller*

## June 8

**The best dreams happen when you're awake.**
*Cherie Gilderbloom*

## June 9

**The road to Easy Street goes through the sewer.**
*John Madden*

## June 10

**When you win, say nothing, when you lose, say less.**
*Paul Brown*

## June 11

**In the depth of winter, I finally learned that within me there lay an invincible summer.**
*Albert Camus*

## June 12

**Nothing diminishes anxiety faster than action.**
*Walter Anderson*

## June 13

**Failure is the opportunity to begin again more intelligently.**

*Henry Ford*

## June 14

**Positive anything is better than negative nothing.**

*Elbert Hubbard*

## June 15

**Absence destroys small passions and increases great ones, as the wind extinguishes tapers and kindles fires.**

*Anon*

## June 16

**You see things; and you say 'Why?' But I dream things that never were; and I say 'Why not?'**

*George Bernard Shaw*

## June 17

**The journey is the reward.**

*Chinese Proverb*

## June 18

**Always listen to the experts. They'll tell you what can't be done and why. Then do it.**

*Robert Heinlein*

## June 19

It is one of the most beautiful
compensations of this life that no man
can sincerely try to help another
without helping himself.
*Ralph Waldo Emerson*

## June 20

The reasonable man adapts himself to
the world; the unreasonable one
persists in trying to adapt the world to
himself. Therefore, all progress
depends on the unreasonable man.
*George Bernard Shaw*

## June 21

Do not confuse motion and progress. A
rocking horse keeps moving but does
not make any progress.
*Alfred A. Montapert*

## June 22

The minute you settle for less than you
deserve, you get even less than you
settled for.
*Maureen Dowd*

## June 23

The future belongs to those who
believe in the beauty of their dreams.
*Eleanor Roosevelt*

## June 24

**Thought is action in rehearsal.**
*Sigmund Freud*

## June 25

**When our memories outweigh our dreams, we have grown old.**
*Bill Clinton*

## June 26

**Once you learn to read, you will be forever free.**
*Frederick Douglas*

## June 27

**A book is a dream that you hold in your hand.**
*Neil Gaiman*

## June 28

**Setting an example is not the main means of influencing others; it is the only means.**
*Albert Einstein*

## June 29

**A book is a device to ignite the imagination.**
*Alan Bennett*

## June 30

**In response to those who say to stop dreaming and face reality, I say keep dreaming and make reality.**
*Kristian Kan*

# JULY

## July 1

Why do men like me want sons?' he wondered. 'It must be because they hope in their poor beaten souls that these new men, who are their blood, will do the things they were not strong enough nor wise enough nor brave enough to do. It is rather like another chance at life; like a new bag of coins at a table of luck after your fortune is gone.'
*John Steinbeck*

## July 2

Like all great travelers, I have seen more than I remember, and remember more than I have seen.
*Benjamin Disraeli*

## July 3

The aim of an argument or discussion should not be victory, but progress.
*Joseph Joubert*

## July 4

Simplicity is the ultimate sophistication.
*Leonardo da Vinci*

## July 5

Strive for progress, not perfection.
*Anon*

## July 6

If your chasing money you will be
running all your life. If you are chasing
dreams, you will be living all your life.
*Tony Gaskins.*

## July 7

Change the changeable, accept the
unchangeable, and remove yourself
from the unacceptable.
*Denis Waitley*

## July 8

The secret of change is to focus all of
your energy, not on fighting the old, but
on building the new.
*Socrates*

## July 9

The mystery of life is not a problem to
be solved but a reality to be
experienced.
*Art Van Der Leeuw*

## July 10

Don't let the past steal your present.
*Cherralea Morgen*

## July 11

To create more positive results in your
life, replace 'if only' with 'next time'.
*Celestine Chua*

## July 12

**Make no small plans for they have no power to stir the soul.**
*Niccolo Machiavelli*

## July 13

**History shows us that the people who end up changing the world – the great political, social, scientific, technological, artistic, even sports revolutionaries – are always nuts, until they are right, and then they are geniuses.**
*John Eliot*

## July 14

**I am not my memories. I am my dreams.**
*Terry Hostetler*

## July 15

**All great changes are preceded by chaos.**
*Deepak Chopra*

## July 16

**In life, as in football, you won't go far unless you know where the goalposts are.**
*Arnold H. Glasgow*

## July 17

Confidence comes not from always being right but not fearing to be wrong. Confident people take risk, take a chance, make a change and make breakthrough. Confidence is the foundation of great achievement.
*Anil Sinha*

## July 18

In order to be walked over, you have to be lying down.
*Celestine Chua*

## July 19

I have no special talents. I am only passionately curious.
*Albert Einstein*

## July 20

A Quitter never wins – and – a Winner never quits.
*Napoleon Hill*

## July 21

The major difference between the big shot and the little shot is the big shot is just a little shot who kept on shooting.
*Zig Ziglar*

## July 22

**The man who does not read good books
has no advantage over the man who
can't read them.**
*Mark Twain*

## July 23

**Little minds have little worries; big
minds have no time for worries.**
*Ralph Waldo Emerson*

## July 24

**Don't say you don't have enough time.
You have exactly the same number of
hours per day that were given to Helen
Keller, Pasteur, Michelangelo, Mother
Teresa, Leonardo da Vinci, Thomas
Jefferson, and Albert Einstein.**
*H. Jackson Brown, Jr.*

## July 25

**I hear and I forget. I see and I
remember. I do and I understand.**
*Confucius*

## July 26

**The positive thinker sees the invisible,
feels the intangible, and achieves the
impossible.**
*Anon*

## July 27

**Instead of thinking outside the box, get rid of the box.**
*Deepak Chopra*

## July 28

**Management is doing things right; leadership is doing the right things.**
*Peter F. Drucker*

## July 29

**Only mediocrity is sure of itself, so take risks, and do what you really want to do.**
*Paulo Coelho*

## July 30

**People seem not to see that their opinion of the world is also a confession of character.**
*Ralph Waldo Emerson*

## July 31

**If you want happiness for an hour - take a nap.**
**If you want happiness for a day -**
**go fishing. If you want happiness for a month - get married. If you want happiness for a year – inherit a fortune. If you want happiness for a lifetime help others.**
*Chinese proverb*

# AUGUST

## August 1

There is only one way to happiness and that is to cease worrying about things which are beyond the power of our will.
*Epictetus*

## August 2

Sometimes your joy is the source of your smile, but sometimes your smile can be the source of your joy.
*Thich Nhat Hanh*

## August 3

Love is that condition in which the happiness of another person is essential to your own.
*Robert A. Heinlein*

## August 4

Happy people plan actions, they don't plan results.
*Dennis Waitley*

## August 5

Time you enjoy wasting is not wasted time.
*Marthe Troly-Curtin*

## August 6

Happiness is having a large, loving, caring, close-knit family in another city.
*George Burns*

## August 7

The pleasure which we most rarely
experience gives us greatest delight.
*Epictetus*

## August 8

Motivation is what gets you started.
Habit is what keeps you going.
*Jim Rohn*

## August 9

For many men, the acquisition of
wealth does not end their troubles, it
only changes them.
*Seneca*

## August 10

A table, a chair, a bowl of fruit and a
violin; what else does a man need to be
happy?
*Albert Einstein*

## August 11

Happy he who learns to bear what he
cannot change.
*Friedrich Schiller*

## August 12

Happiness is a how; not a what. A
talent, not an object.
*Herman Hesse*

## August 13

No act of kindness, no matter how
small, is ever wasted.
*Aesop*

## August 14

The best years of your life are the ones
in which you decide your problems are
your own. You do not blame them on
your mother, the ecology, or the
president. You realize that you control
your own destiny.
*Albert Ellis*

## August 15

I, not events, have the power to make
me happy or unhappy today. I can
choose which it shall be. Yesterday is
dead, tomorrow hasn't arrived yet. I
have just one day, today, and I'm going
to be happy in it.
*Groucho Marx*

## August 16

Worry never robs tomorrow of its
sorrow. It only saps today of its joy.
*Leo Buscaglia*

## August 17

Be happy with what you have. Be
excited about what you want.
*Alan Cohen*

## August 18

Happiness always looks small while you hold it in your hands, but let it go, and you learn at once how big and precious it is.
*Maxim Gorky*

## August 19

Twenty years from now you will be more disappointed by the things that you didn't do than by the ones you did do. So throw off the bowlines. Sail away from the safe harbor. Catch the trade winds in your sails. Explore. Dream. Discover.
*Mark Twain*

## August 20

Plenty of people miss their share of happiness, not because they never found it, but because they didn't stop to enjoy it.
*William Feather*

## August 21

I have found opportunities do not come to those who wait. They are captured by those who attack.
*William Danforth*

## August 22

Go as far as you can see; when you get there, you'll be able to see farther.
*J. P. Morgan*

## August 23

Think big thoughts but relish small pleasures.
*H. Jackson Brown Jr*

## August 24

Pain is temporary. Quitting is forever
*Lance Armstrong*

## August 25

There are two ways of spreading light: to be the candle, or the mirror that reflects it.
*Edith Wharton*

## August 26

Hate. It has caused a lot of problems in this world but has not solved one yet.
*Maya Angelou*

## August 27

An attitude of positive expectation is the mark of the superior personality.
*Brian Tracy*

## August 28

**We must accept finite disappointment, but never lose infinite hope.**
*Martin Luther King Jr.*

## August 29

**We don't see things as they are, we see them as we are.**
*Anais Nin*

## August 30

**Life has many ways of testing a person's will, either by having nothing happen at all or by having everything happen all at once.**
*Paulo Coelho*

## August 31

**The past has no power over the present moment.**
*Eckhart Tolle*

# SEPTEMBER

## September 1

**We are what we seem to be**
*Willard Gaylin*

## September 2

**There is little difference in people, but that little difference makes a big difference. The little difference is attitude. The big difference is whether it is positive or negative.**
*W. Clement Stone*

## September 3

**Men are moved by two levers only: fear and self-interest.**
*Napoleon Bonaparte*

## September 4

**Do not use a hatchet to remove a fly from your friend's forehead.**
*Chinese Proverb*

## September 5

**We are responsible for what we are, and whatever we wish ourselves to be, we have the power to make ourselves.**
*Swami Vivekananda*

## September 6

**If you want to make your dreams come true, the first thing you have to do is wake up.**

*J.M. Power*

## September 7

**Deliberation is the action of many; action is the function of one.**

*Charles de Gaulle*

## September 8

**Only when it is dark enough, can you see the stars.**

*Charles A Beard*

## September 9

**Don't be afraid to stand for what you believe in, even if that means standing alone.**

*Andy Biersack*

## September 10

**When it is obvious the goals cannot be reached, don't adjust the goals, adjust the actions.**

*Confucius*

## September 11

You yourself, as much as anybody in the entire universe deserve your love and affection.

*Buddha*

## September 12

Today is a new beginning, a chance to turn your failures into achievements and your sorrows into so goods. No room for excuses.

*Joel Brown*

## September 13

The next time you feel slightly uncomfortable with the pressure in your life, remember no pressure, no diamonds. Pressure is a part of success.

*Eric Thomas*

## September 14

When you say "It's hard", it actually means "I'm not strong enough to fight for it". Stop saying its hard. Think positive!

*Anon*

## September 15

Don't worry about failures, worry about the chances you miss when you don't even try.

*Jack Canfield*

## September 16

The only thing that stands between you and your dream is the will to try and the belief that it is actually possible.
*Joel Brown*

## September 17

Though no one can go back and make a brand new start, anyone can start from now and make a brand new ending.
*Carl Bard*

## September 18

I do not believe in taking the right decision, I take a decision and make it right.
*Muhammad Ali Jinnah*

## September 19

A man who views the world the same at fifty as he did at twenty has wasted thirty years of his life.
*Muhammed Ali*

## September 20

Don't be afraid of your fears. They're not there to scare you. They're there to let you know that something is worth it.
*C. JoyBell C.*

## September 21

The first step toward success is taken when you refuse to be a captive of the environment in which you first find yourself.
*Mark Caine*

## September 22

There is no chance, no destiny, no fate, that can hinder or control the firm resolve of a determined soul.
*Ella Wheeler Wilcox*

## September 23

Success is ... knowing your purpose in life, growing to reach your maximum potential, and sowing seeds that benefit others.
*John C. Maxwell*

## September 24

Most of the important things in the world have been accomplished by people who have kept on trying when there seemed to be no help at all.
*Dale Carnegie*

## September 25

You measure the size of the accomplishment by the obstacles you had to overcome to reach your goals.
*Booker T. Washington*

## September 26

**It is better to fail in originality than to succeed in limitation.**

*Herman Melville*

## September 27

**Failure is the condiment that gives success its flavor.**

*Truman Capote*

## September 28

**You may have to fight a battle more than once to win it.**

*Margaret Thatcher*

## September 29

**Definiteness of purpose is the starting point of all achievement.**

*W. Clement Stone*

## September 30

**I've learned that people will forget what you said, people will forget what you did, but people will never forget how you made them feel.**

*Maya Angelou*

# OCTOBER

## October 1

We must believe that we are gifted for something, and that this thing, at whatever cost, must be attained.

*Marie Curie*

## October 2

Remember no one can make you feel inferior without your consent.

*Eleanor Roosevelt*

## October 3

Change is inevitable. Change is constant.

*Benjamin Disraeli*

## October 4

The question isn't who is going to let me; it's who is going to stop me.

*Ayn Rand*

## October 5

Any change, even a change for the better, is always accompanied by drawbacks and discomforts.

*Arnold Bennett*

## October 6

The price of doing the same old thing is far higher than the price of change.

*Bill Clinton*

## October 7

**It's not who you are that holds you back. It's who you think you're not.**

*Anon*

## October 8

**If opportunity doesn't knock, build a door.**

*Milton Berle*

## October 9

**Very little is needed to make a happy life; it is all within yourself, in your way of thinking.**

*Marcus Aurelius*

## October 10

**Don't wait around for other people to be happy for you. Any happiness you get, you've got to make yourself.**

*Alice Walker*

## October 11

**If you're presenting yourself with confidence, you can pull off pretty much anything.**

*Katy Perry*

## October 12

**Your friends will believe in your potential; your enemies will make you live up to it.**
*Tim Fargo*

## October 13

**A ship is safe in harbor, but that's not what ships are for.**
*William G.T. Shedd*

## October 14

**We choose to go to the moon and do these other things, not because they are easy, but because they are hard.**
*John Fitzgerald Kennedy*

## October 15

**Always remember you are braver than you believe, stronger than you seem, smarter than you think and twice as beautiful as you've ever imagined.**
*Dr. Seuss*

## October 16

**Education is not the filling of a pail, but the lighting of a fire.**
*W.B. Yeats*

## October 17

People often become what they believe
themselves to be. If I believe I cannot
do something, it makes me incapable of
doing it. But when I believe I can, then I
acquire the ability to do it even if I
didn't have it in the beginning.
*Mahatma Gandhi*

## October 18

Failure is simply the opportunity to
begin again, this time more
intelligently.
*Henry Ford*

## October 19

Opportunity is missed by people
because it is dressed in overalls and
looks like work.
*Thomas Alva Edison*

## October 20

It has been said that a person may have
ten years of experience, or one year of
experience repeated ten times.
*Yukiso Yamamoto*

## October 21

Talent is luck. The important thing in
life is courage.
*Woody Allen*

## October 22

Courage isn't having the strength to go on – it is going on when you don't have strength.
*Napoleon Bonaparte*

## October 23

When you realize how perfect everything is, you will tilt your head back and laugh at the sky.
*Buddha*

## October 24

Don't ask yourself what the world needs. Ask yourself what makes you come alive, and then go and do that, because what the world needs is people that have come alive.
*Howard Thurman*

## October 25

Today I do what others won't, so that tomorrow I can accomplish what others don't.
*Jerry Rice*

## October 26

Whatever the mind of man can conceive and believe, it can achieve.
*Napoleon Hill*

## October 27

**If you hear a voice within you say "you cannot paint," then by all means paint and that voice will be silenced.**
*Vincent Van Gogh*

## October 28

**What we achieve inwardly will change outer reality.**
*Plutarch*

## October 29

**Dream big and dare to fail.**
*Norman Vaughan*

## October 30

**Without inspiration the best powers of the mind remain dormant. There is a fuel in us which needs to be ignited with sparks.**
*Johann Gottfried Von Herder*

## October 31

**Nothing will ever be attempted if all possible objections must first be overcome.**
*Samuel Johnson*

# NOVEMBER

## November 1

We are all inventors, each sailing out
on a voyage of discovery, guided each
by a private chart, of which there is no
duplicate. The world is all gates, all
opportunities.
*Ralph Waldo Emerson*

## November 2

Strong lives are motivated by dynamic
purposes.
*Kenneth Hildebrand*

## November 3

Nothing is worth more than this day.
You cannot relive yesterday.
Tomorrow is still beyond our reach.
*Johann Wolfgang Von Goethe*

## November 4

In any project the important factor is
your belief. Without belief, there can be
no successful outcome.
*William James*

## November 5

We are still captains of our souls.
*Winston Churchill*

## November 6

**People throw stones at you and you convert them into milestones.**
*Sachin Tendulkar*

## November 7

**An attitude of positive expectation is the mark of the superior personality.**
*Brian Tracy*

## November 8

**With everything that has happened to you, you can either feel sorry for yourself or treat what has happened as a gift. Everything is either an opportunity to grow or an obstacle to keep you from growing. You get to choose.**
*Dr. Wayne W Dyer*

## November 9

**Your success in life isn't based on your ability to simply change. It is based on your ability to change faster than your competition, customers, and business.**
*Mark Sanborn*

## November 10

**If you can dream it, then you can achieve it. You will get all you want in life if you help enough other people get what they want.**
*Zig Ziglar*

## November 11

**Learning is a gift. Even when pain is your teacher.**

*Maya Watson*

## November 12

**I may not have gone where I intended to go, but I think I have ended up where I needed to be.**

*Douglas Adams*

## November 13

**Believing in negative thoughts is the single greatest obstruction to success.**

*Charles F. Glassman*

## November 14

**Energy and persistence conquer all things.**

*Benjamin Franklin*

## November 15

**Don't let what you cannot do interfere with what you can do.**

*John R. Wooden*

## November 16

**Change is the law of life. And those who look only to the past or present are certain to miss the future.**

*John F. Kennedy*

## November 17

**Be like the flower that gives fragrance
even to the hand that crushes it.**
*Ali Ibn Abi Talib*

## November 18

**Not until we are lost, do we begin to
find ourselves.**
*Henry David Thoreau*

## November 19

**Believe with all of your heart that you
will do what you were made to do.**
*Orison Swett Marden*

## November 20

**If you want light to come into your life,
you need to stand where it is shining.**
*Guy Finley*

## November 21

**We are all here for some special reason.
Stop being a prisoner of your past.
Become the architect of your future.**
*Robin Sharma*

## November 22

**All you can change is yourself, but
sometimes that changes everything.**
*Gary W Goldstein*

## November 23

**Take chances, make mistakes. That's how you grow. Pain nourishes your courage. You have to fail in order to practice being brave.**

*Mary Tyler Moore*

## November 24

**The difference between stumbling blocks and stepping stones is how you use them.**

*Anon*

## November 25

**You are never too old to set another goal or dream a new dream.**

*C.S Lewis*

## November 26

**If you can change your mind, you can change your life.**

*William James*

## November 27

**All things are difficult before they are easy.**

*Thomas Fuller*

## November 28

Be soft. Do not let the world make you hard. Do not let pain make you hate. Do not let the bitterness steal your sweetness. Take pride that even though the rest of the world may disagree, you still believe it to be a beautiful place.
*Kurt Vonnegut*

## November 29

The best way to gain self-confidence is to do what you are afraid to do.
*Anon*

## November 30

There is no such thing as failure. There are only results.
*Tony Robbins*

# DECEMBER

### December 1

**Start where you are. Use what you have.**
**Do what you can.**
*Arthur Ashe*

### December 2

**You can't build a reputation on what**
**you are going to do.**
*Henry Ford*

### December 3

**What you do today can improve all**
**your tomorrows.**
*Ralph Marston*

### December 4

**Mental attitude is more important than**
**mental capacity.**
*Walter Dill Scott*

### December 5

**Kites rise highest against the wind; not**
**with it.**
*Winston Churchill*

### December 6

**Those who cannot change their minds**
**cannot change anything.**
*George Bernard Shaw*

## December 7

**The best way out is always through.**

*Robert Frost*

## December 8

**No pleasure is worth giving up for the sake of two more years in a geriatric home in Weston super Mare.**

*Kingsley Amis*

## December 9

**Keep your eyes on the stars, and your feet on the ground.**

*Theodore Roosevelt*

## December 10

**The only way of finding the limits of the possible is by going beyond them into the impossible.**

*Arthur C. Clarke*

## December 11

**To be a great champion you must believe you are the best. If you're not, pretend you are.**

*Muhammad Ali*

## December 12

**Attitude determines altitude.**

*Anon*

## December 13

You have to learn the rules of the game.
And then you have to play better than
anyone else.
*Albert Einstein*

## December 14

To different minds, the same world is a
hell, and a heaven.
*Ralph Waldo Emerson*

## December 15

Optimism means expecting the best,
but confidence means knowing how to
handle the worst. Never make a move if
you are merely optimistic.
*Max Gunther*

## December 16

A man is what he thinks about all day
long.
*Ralph Waldo Emerson*

## December 17

A man's growth is seen in the
successive choirs of his friends.
*Ralph Waldo Emerson*

## December 18

With ordinary talent and extraordinary
perseverance, all things are attainable.
*Thomas Foxwell Buxton*

## December 19

Happiness is not in the mere possession of money; it lies in the joy of achievement, in the thrill of creative effort.

*Franklin D. Roosevelt*

## December 20

The unhappy derive comfort from the misfortunes of others.

*Aesop*

## December 21

Of all forms of caution, caution in love is perhaps the most fatal to true happiness.

*Bertrand Russell*

## December 22

The most beautiful people we have known are those who have known defeat, known suffering, known struggle, known loss, and have found their way out of the depths. These persons have an appreciation, a sensitivity and an understanding of life that fills them with compassion, gentleness, and a deep loving concern. Beautiful people do not just happen.

*Elizabeth Kubler-Ross*

## December 23

Life is really simple, but we insist on making it complicated.
*Confucius*

## December 24

Just because it didn't last forever, doesn't mean it wasn't worth your while.
*Anon*

## December 25

Happiness is something that comes into our lives through doors we don't even remember leaving open.
*Rose Lane*

## December 26

It was only a sunny smile, and little it cost in the giving, but like morning light it scattered the night and made the day worth living.
*F. Scott Fitzgerald*

## December 27

Gratitude is a vaccine, an antitoxin, and an antiseptic.
*John Henry Jowett*

## December 28

When things go wrong, don't go with them.
*Elvis Presley*

### December 29

**Let us be grateful to the people who make us happy; they are the charming gardeners who make our souls blossom.**

*Marcel Proust*

### December 30

**Once you choose hope, anything's possible.**

*Christopher Reeve*

### December 31

**Optimism is a happiness magnet. If you stay positive, good things and good people will be drawn to you.**

*Mary Lou Retton*

## ONE LAST THING...

If you enjoyed this book or found it useful I'd be very grateful if you'd post a short review on Amazon. Your support really does make a difference and I read all the reviews personally so I can get your feedback and make this book even better.

Many thanks for your support

Made in the USA
Las Vegas, NV
28 April 2024

89260522R00059